Daughters of Zion Prayer Series Volume 9

The DZM Prayer Manual

by
Celie Anazodo

Daughters of Zion Prayer Series Volume 9: The DZM Prayer Manual
by Celie Anazodo

Cover design by Daughters of Zion Ministry

First edition, printed in the United States of America

© 2020 by Daughters of Zion Ministry, all rights reserved

No portion of this book may be reproduced in any form without permission from Daughters of Zion Ministry

For reproduction permission, please email Celie Anazodo at dzmpraise@yahoo.com

Some scripture taken from the Holy Bible, New International Version® © 1973, 1978, 1986 by International Bible Society. Used by permission of Zondervan®.

Some scripture taken from the Holy Bible, New King James Version ® © 1979, 1980, 1982, 1999 by Thomas Nelson, Inc. Used by Permission of Thomas Nelson, Inc.

Bible versions accessed through www.Biblegateway.com

ISBN: 978-1-949720-53-2

Daughters of Zion Prayer Series Volume 9
The Prayer Manual

Contact DZM

Please address your email to Celie Anazodo and send it to dzmpraise@yahoo.com.

We would like you to share your testimony with us at dzmpraise@yahoo.com.

Please visit us at www.dzministry.webs.com.

**Daughters of Zion Prayer Series Volume 9
The Prayer Manual**

Scriptural Basis

Ezekiel 22:30

> "So I sought for a man among them
> who would make a wall,
> and stand in the gap before Me
> on behalf of the land,
> that I should not destroy it;
> but I found no one."

Isaiah 62:1; 6-7

"For Zion's sake I will not hold My peace,
And for Jerusalem's sake I will not rest,
Until her righteousness goes forth as brightness,
And her salvation as a lamp that burns."

"I have set watchmen on your walls, O Jerusalem;
they shall never hold their peace day or night.
You who make mention of the Lord,
do not keep silent,
And give Him no rest till He establishes
And till He makes Jerusalem a praise in the earth."

**Daughters of Zion Prayer Series Volume 9
The Prayer Manual**

Preface

This Prayer Manual is a simple and yet a profound strategic small prayer book that inspired believers in Christ Jesus to pray strategically through this book. It teaches the readers on how to present their prayer request to God, from the beginning to an end. This book is fashioned as a weapon to raise end time prayer warriors to pray through with faith and in the word of God.

Hannah prayed a strategic prayer to God when she was provoked by her rival severely, to make her miserable, because the Lord had closed her womb. (I Samuel 1:6)

"She cried out to God, and made a vow and said, "O Lord of hosts, if You will indeed look on the affliction of Your maidservant and remember me, and not forget Your maidservant, but will give Your maidservant a male child, then I will give him to the Lord all

Daughters of Zion Prayer Series Volume 9
The Prayer Manual

the days of his life, and no razor shall come upon his head." (1 Samuel 1:11)

Her prayer request was strategic. She wanted a male child and that was what she prayed for. Then she made a vow that she will give him back to the Lord all the days of his life. Her prayer was answered and she fulfilled her vow to the Lord.

This book is a spiritual bulldozer when planted in the hand of a prayer warrior, written carefully step-by-step prayer book that starts with a prayer of praise, confession of sins, binding spiritual wickedness, invitation to the Holy Spirit, then petition/supplication and finally DZM prophetic prayer ministries member's testimonies.

My prayer is for God to release upon you a spirit of prayer so that you will have a breakthrough, divine encounter with the Holy Spirit and all your prayers answered in Jesus name. Amen!

**Daughters of Zion Prayer Series Volume 9
The Prayer Manual**

Acknowledgements

My greatest acknowledgement goes to my Father in heaven, Who said, "Ask, and it will be given to you; seek, and you will find; knock, and it will be opened to you. For where two or three are gathered together in My name, I am there in the midst of them." (Matthew 7:7; 18:20)

Special thanks goes to all the members of the Daughters of Zion Prophetic Prayer Ministry who dial in faithfully every Saturday morning, from all walks of life. Thank you for standing in prayer with our Lord and Savior Jesus, Who sits at the right hand of the Father, interceding for us. May the Lord bless you and keep you all as we labor in prayer.

Daughters of Zion Prayer Series Volume 9
The Prayer Manual

Contents

Chapter 1
Prayer of Praise 1

Chapter 2
Prayer of Thanksgiving 4

Chapter 3
Prayer of Confession of Sin 8

Chapter 4
Prayer to Bind Spiritual Wickedness in
Heavenly Places 11

Chapter 5
Invitation of the Holy Spirit 14

Chapter 6
Prayer of Petition/Supplication 18

Chapter 7
Testimonies 25

**Daughters of Zion Prayer Series Volume 9
The Prayer Manual**

1

Prayer of Praise

Psalm 113:1-4 (NKJV)

"Praise the Lord! Praise, O servants of the Lord, Praise the name of the Lord! Blessed be the name of the Lord From this time forth and forevermore! From the rising of the sun to its going down. The Lord's name is to be praised. The Lord is high above all nations, His glory above the heavens."

The scripture says it's good to praise the Lord for His goodness and mercies, so what a better way to start prayer by praising God for all He has done. He is the lilies of the valleys, ancient of days, healer, deliverer, the alpha and the omega, the beginning and the end, who was and He is to come. When King Jehoshaphat faced a great multitude of armies coming against him from Syria, He set himself to seek the Lord, proclaimed a fast throughout all Judah. He prayed in the mist of Judah and Jerusalem, "O our God, will You not judge them? For we have no power against this great multitude that is now coming against us; nor do we know what to do, but our eyes are upon You."(2 Chronicles 20:12)

Then the Spirit of the Lord came upon Jahaziel, he prophesied and asked them not to be afraid or dismayed because of this great multitude for the battle is not theirs but God's.

They positioned themselves, King Jehoshaphat appointed those who should sing to the Lord and praise Him, "Praising the Lord, for His mercy endures forever." When they began to sing and to praise, the Lord set ambushes against their enemies and they were defeated. The enemies helped to destroy one another. The Psalmist tells us to make a joyful noise to the Lord, come before His presence with singing and enter His courts with praise. A brilliant way to start prayer is to enter His presence with praise. It will get His attention, for when praises go up, His blessings come down. God inhabits in the praises of His people. Therefore, when you start to pray, start with praises.

Daughters of Zion Prayer Series Volume 9
The Prayer Manual

Praise Him in the morning. Praise Him in the evening. Praise Him when the sun goes down. Praise Him from the rising of the sun to the going down of the set. Praise Him for what He has done and what He is going to do. Praise Him for all the battles He has won for you, for that breakthrough he has granted you. Praise Him for healing you and providing for you. And watch Him do more for you. Hallelujah!

Prayer
Pause for ten minutes and give God praise. Worship him with seven songs and pray in the Holy Spirt!

Daughters of Zion Prayer Series Volume 9
The Prayer Manual

2

Prayer of Thanksgiving

Psalm 100:4-5 (NKJV)

"Enter into His gates with thanksgiving, And into His courts with praise. Be thankful to Him, and bless His name. For the Lord is good; His mercy is everlasting, and His truth endures to all generations."

After you have come before His presence with singing and have entered His courts with praise, the next step is to enter into his gates with thanksgiving. It's only as we approach God in this manner that we will have access into His Presence.

This is where you begin to thank God for all He has done for you. For saving you, your love ones, and what he is about to do. Psalm 103:2-5 says, "Bless the Lord, O my soul; And all that is within me, bless His holy name! Bless the Lord, O my soul, And forget not all His benefits: Who forgives all your iniquities,

Daughters of Zion Prayer Series Volume 9
The Prayer Manual

Who heals all your diseases, Who redeems your life from destruction, Who crowns you with lovingkindness and tender mercies, Who satisfies your mouth with good things, So that your youth is renewed like the eagle's." This is a heart that is thankful and grateful to the Lord for all the benefits they enjoy, knowing that all good things come from Him.

Giving thanks is a biblical way to release the power of God. When Jesus fed the 5,000 on a hillside, note He did not pray for the multiplication miracle. He merely gave thanks. "Jesus then took the loaves, gave thanks, and distributed to those who were seated as much as they wanted. He did the same with the fish." (John 6:11)

This thanks, by itself, released a divine power that turned the elements of the little boy's humble meal into an overabundant one for 5,000 men — to say nothing of the women and children present. Likewise, when Jesus stood before the tomb of Lazarus, he didn't pray a prayer of petition. He simple thanked the father that He always heard Him. "So they took away the stone. Then Jesus looked up and said, 'Father, I thank you that you have heard me. I knew that you always hear me, but I said this for the benefit of the people standing here, that they may believe that you sent me.'" (John 11:41-42)

Giving thanks is the will of God in any and all situations! Understanding this key principle will have a direct hearing on how we pray. "Do not be anxious about anything, but in every situation, by prayer and petition, with thanksgiving, present your requests to God." (Philippians 4:6)

Sometimes we are tempted to look at our situation and think, what do I have to thank God for? There may seem to be nothing for which you can express thanks.

The Psalmist has given us at least three reasons to thank and praise that are not affected by our current circumstances.

First, the Lord is good. Second, His love endures forever! And third, His faithfulness continues throughout all generations!

All three of these reasons are eternal, unchanging facts. If we really believe these truths, then we have no alternative but to thank God for them continually. If we omit thanksgiving and praise in our prayer, we will be like the nine lepers who did not return to praise the Lord for their healing.

One of them, when he saw he was healed, came back, praising God in a loud voice. He threw himself at Jesus' feet and thanked him — and he was a Samaritan. Jesus asked, "Were not all ten cleansed? Where are the other nine? Has no one returned to give praise to God except this foreigner?"

Then he said to him, "Rise and go; your faith has made you well." All ten lepers were healed physically, but only the one who returned to give thanks was healed spiritually! Returning to give thanks set an eternal seal upon him. The best ways to begin prayer is by always beginning with praise and thanksgiving. When we focus on God and His Love for us, it will keep us focused on what is truly important. Therefore, when you pray, don't omit your grateful offering of praise and thanksgiving. Amen!

Prayer
Thank God for at least ten things He has done for you!

**Daughters of Zion Prayer Series Volume 9
The Prayer Manual**

Prayer of Confession of Sins

Proverbs 28:13 (NIV)

"Whoever conceals their sins does not prosper, but the one who confesses and renounces them finds mercy."

After you have praised and given thanks, the next step is to go into confession of sins, for the one who confesses and renounces their sins will be forgiven. Repent of any unforgiveness/bitterness/anger/wickedness, fornication/stealing /fraud and anything that does not bring glory to the father, "The sacrifice of the wicked is an abomination to the Lord; but the prayer of the upright is a delight."

If you are living in sin, your prayer fasting is an abomination unto God. We have to humble ourselves to pray, seek the face of God and turn away from our wicked ways. When we do that, three things will happen:

Daughters of Zion Prayer Series Volume 9
The Prayer Manual

First, the Lord will hear from heaven! Second, He will forgive your sin! And third, He will heal the land. "Blessed is the one whose transgressions are forgiven, whose sins are covered. Blessed is the one whose sin the Lord does not count against them and in whose spirit is no deceit." (Psalm 32:1-2)

We have to ask, seek and knock so that the gate of our prayer will be opened to us. Sin is a blocker; it will block the gate to access the gate of breakthrough to prayer. Before you move forward with your prayer, you have to ask God to forgive you of your sins and plead the blood of Jesus. Remember, the blood Jesus shed for you on the cross of calvary, His death, burial and resurrection on the third day.

Every one of us shall give account of himself to God, for all have sinned and come short of the glory of God. Deploy, the blood of Jesus a powerful weapon for cleansing, saving, healing, redeeming, sanctification and purification. Blood of Jesus is a weapon to give you access to the throne of God. We overcame Satan by the blood of the Lamb and by the word of our testimony. Use the blood of Jesus to cancel any known and unknown sins. Employ the blood of Jesus to cover your prayer vicinity, wash, cleanse and cancel every evil pronouncement and evil covenant made against you.

Prayer
Confess your sins!

Right now Lord, I confess my sins of lying, lust, jealousy, envy, anger, stealing, greed, sexual immorality, impurity, prayerlessness, evil thoughts and evil desires. The bible says if we confess our sins, He is faithful and just and will forgive us our sins and purify us from all unrighteousness.

4

Prayer to Bind Spiritual Wickedness in Heavenly Places

Matthew 16:19 (NIV)

"I will give you the keys of the kingdom of heaven; whatever you bind on earth will be bound in heaven, and whatever you loose on earth will be loosed in heaven."

This is the fourth step: you bind spiritual wickedness in the heavenly that detains prayer. Daniel prayed and fasted for three weeks; however, the answer to his prayers did not come because the prince of a Persian kingdom resisted it for 21 days, to then Michael, and one of the chief princes came to help. The key represents authority. You have the key to gain access to your house or to your car; therefore, you have to bind Satan's interference to your prayer. You have to possess access to the throne by taking authority over every foul spirit. The bible says

Daughters of Zion Prayer Series Volume 9
The Prayer Manual

He has given us authority to bind and to loose.

Apostle Paul said in 1 Corinthians 16:9, "For a great and effective door has opened to me, and there are many adversaries."

Take authority over every adversary foul spirit/contrary spirit/spirit of disaccord/confusion from the camp of the enemy/every arrow/fiery dart that will hinder your prayer. For it is written that we do not wrestle against flesh and blood, but against principalities, against powers, against the rulers of the darkness of this age, against spiritual hosts of wickedness in the heavenly places. "For the weapons of our warfare are not carnal but mighty in God for pulling down of strongholds. (2 Corinthians 10:4)

Casting down imaginations and every thing that exalts itself against the knowledge of God, and bringing into captivity every thought to the obedience of Christ.

In the mighty name of Jesus, take authority over the territorial atmosphere of your prayer. Soak the vicinity of your prayer in the blood of Jesus. Bind all anti-prayer spirits, command

Daughters of Zion Prayer Series Volume 9
The Prayer Manual

all depressive thoughts, spirit of heaviness to be uprooted in Jesus' name.

Take authority in the mighty name of Jesus; for we have been given the authority to trample on serpents and scorpions, and over all the power of the enemy, and nothing shall by any means hurt you.

Prayer
Now, begin to bind and loose. Power of life and death are in your tongue. Use it!

**Daughters of Zion Prayer Series Volume 9
The Prayer Manual**

5

Invitation of the Holy Spirit

Acts 2:17 (NKJV)

> "And it shall come to pass in the last days, says God, That I will pour out of My Spirit on all flesh; Your sons and your daughters shall prophesy, Your young men shall see visions, Your old men shall dream dreams."

This is the fifth step where you invite the presence of the Holy Spirit to overrule every presence. You need the presence of the Holy Spirit to empower you to pray through, lead and guide you to know what to pray and how to pray. The Holy Spirit is our advocate, helper, spirit of truth, our teacher, reminder. He guides us to all truth. He glorifies God (John 16:4), He convicts (John 16:8), He regenerate us, He lives in us, He seals the believers, He prompts us, He empower us, He gives life to our mortal bodies, and gives us special gifts, He enables the believers to

Daughters of Zion Prayer Series Volume 9
The Prayer Manual

produce the fruit of the spirit, He is our helper.

"But the Helper, the Holy Spirit, whom the Father will send in My name, He will teach you all things, and bring to your remembrance all things that I said to you." (John 14:26)

"However, when He, the Spirit of truth, has come, He will guide you into all truth; for He will not speak on His own authority, but whatever He hears He will speak; and He will tell you things to come. He will glorify Me, for He will take of what is Mine and declare it to you. All things that the Father has are Mine. Therefore I said that He will take of Mine and declare it to you." (John 16:13-15)

"The Spirit also helps our weaknesses. For we do not know what we should pray for as we ought, but the Spirit Himself makes intercession for us with groaning's which cannot be uttered." (Romans 8:26)

The Holy Spirit is a "person" and the third person of the Triune God. He is the person of God who lives with us in our time on earth and teaches us a truly know and follow God. The Holy Spirit could be a symbol of a dove, like when Jesus was baptized in River Jordon

Daughters of Zion Prayer Series Volume 9
The Prayer Manual

and he appeared in form of a dove. Or a tongue of fire, like the disciples. Or the divine power that resurrected our Lord Jesus from the grave.

The Holy Spirit is active and effective agent of the Godhead. Even Jesus was anointed with the Holy Spirit and the power to enable Him go about doing good. (Acts 10:38)

Sometimes we acknowledge his power, gift, fruit and characteristics without acknowledging Him, the owner of these gifts. Is only the Holy Spirit that can fill us with God's power to do the work of God. The Holy Spirit, the Spirit of truth, is our advocate, counselor, helper and comforter. If one has a good advocate, he can go to Court with confidence. These and many innumerable things are what the Holy Spirit does in our lives. He dwells in us individually and in our church. The joy of being with the Holy Spirit is that He is everywhere. What we need to do daily and many times a day is just to invite Him to lead and guide us, no matter where we are. If we do so, He will direct and motivate us on how to pray because due to our weaknesses, we do not know how to pray and as a result, he intercedes for us in an inexpressible groaning. (Romans 8:26)

Daughters of Zion Prayer Series Volume 9
The Prayer Manual

Prayer

Invite the Holy Spirit into your spirit now to fill you up with fire just like the day of Pentecost. Ask that your spiritual ears be open so you can hear Him, and your eyes will be open with visions. Fill your mouth to prophesy, give you Spiritual gift, fruit of the spirit and baptize you in the Holy Spirit.

Daughters of Zion Prayer Series Volume 9
The Prayer Manual

6

Prayer of Petition/Supplication

1 Timothy 2:1-3 (NKJV)

"Therefore I exhort first of all that supplications, prayers, intercessions, and giving of thanks be made for all men, for kings and all who are in authority, that we may lead a quiet and peaceable life in all godliness and reverence. For this is good and acceptable in the sight of God our Savior."

After we have praised, given thanks, confessed our sins, bind and invited the presence of the Holy Spirit, it's time to make our request made know to God. Step six is where we begin to intercede for our needs before the Lord.

There is power in praying in the word of God. Jeremiah 23:29 says, "'Is not My word like a fire?" says the Lord "And like a hammer that breaks the rock in pieces?'"

Daughters of Zion Prayer Series Volume 9
The Prayer Manual

In Isaiah 11:2 it is written, "The Spirit of the Lord shall rest upon Him, The Spirit of wisdom and understanding, The Spirit of counsel and might, The Spirit of knowledge and of the fear of the Lord."

Pray
Heavenly Father, may your Spirit rest upon me and my family, Spirit of wisdom and understanding, counsel and might, Spirit of Knowledge and the fear of the Lord in Jesus' name. Amen.

In 3 John 2 it is written, "Beloved, I pray that you may prosper in all things and be in health, just as your soul prospers."

Pray
My God my God, I pray that I will prosper in my health, marriage, job, finances, relationships and in everything that I lay my hand to do in the mighty name of Jesus. Amen.

In Exodus 23:25 it is written, "So you shall serve the Lord your God, and He will bless your bread and your water. And I will take sickness away from the midst of you."

Daughters of Zion Prayer Series Volume 9
The Prayer Manual

Pray

Lift up a bottle of water and pray, Father I declare this water healing water; and turn it to be Blood of Jesus in the mighty name of Jesus.

In Mark 11: 23 it is written, "For assuredly, I say to you, whoever says to this mountain, 'Be removed and be cast into the sea,' and does not doubt in his heart, but believes that those things he says will be done, he will have whatever he says."

Pray

Now speak to your mountains (mountains represents challenges in your life, sickness, failures, financial problems, bareness and stagnation). Command them to be moved in the mighty name of Jesus.

Speak to your body now in the name of Jesus. High blood pressure, diabetes, cancer in my body, hear the word of God and be removed from my body in the mighty name of Jesus. My digestive system, circulatory system, my nervous system, operate in total harmony with each other in Jesus' name.

Sickness and disease, you can't live in my body. My body is the temple of our Lord

Daughters of Zion Prayer Series Volume 9
The Prayer Manual

Jesus. You cannot kill me. Go now into abyss in the mighty name of Jesus. He was bruised for my iniquities, the chastisement of my peace was on him, and by His stripes I am healed.

Power of God, arise and fight this sickness in my body in the name of Jesus.

O voice of God, speak solution into my finances, my marriage, relationships in the mighty name of Jesus.

Fire of God, purse my pursuers, overtake my overtakers and waste the waster in the mighty name of Jesus.

Every conspiracy and Ahithophel Counsel in the heavenliness against my life, my destiny, my job, my ministry, my children and my spouse, scatter by fire in the name of Jesus.

Declarations
There is power released when you speak God's word. Release your faith as you boldly say these declarations. Speak with power and authority. God's words and promises activate divine spiritual forces that bring breakthroughs and manifestations. Now, start speaking: I boldly and authoritatively declare

Daughters of Zion Prayer Series Volume 9
The Prayer Manual

no weapon that is formed or fashioned against me, my family; it shall not prosper in the name of Jesus.

I am strong in the Lord and in the power of His might. I am steadfast and unmovable.

I can do all things through Christ who strengthens me. My strength is renewed like the eagles. God increase my strength; therefore I will not be weary. I speak supernatural strength and energy to my body in Jesus' name.

I will not die but live and declare the works of the Lord. I break chains and bonds of sickness and diseases in the name of Jesus.

I am redeemed from the curse; it no longer has power over me. Jesus has given me power, dominion and authority over sickness and disease.

I proclaim that I am free of sickness and disease and I walk in health, healing and wholeness in the name of Jesus.

I declare I shall not be afraid of the terror by night, nor of the arrow that flies by day, nor of the pestilence that walks in darkness, nor

Daughters of Zion Prayer Series Volume 9
The Prayer Manual

of the destruction that lays waste at noonday. A thousand may fall at your side, and ten thousand at your right hand, but it shall not come near me. Only with my eyes shall I look and see the reward of the wicked. Because you have made the Lord, who is my refuge, Even the Most High, your dwelling place, no evil shall befall me, nor shall any plague come near my dwelling; for He shall give His angels charge over me, to keep me in all my ways. (Psalm 91:5-11)

Action
Take all copies of your bills, taxes, mortgages, school loan, bank loans and anything that represents debt and lay it before the Lord; I speak to you in Jesus' name be paid in full in the mighty name of Jesus.

I now declare that all my debts are paid in full and cancelled in Jesus' name. Amen.

It is written in Matthew 18:18, "Assuredly, I say to you, whatever you bind on earth will be bound in heaven, and whatever you loose on earth will be loosed in heaven." In the mighty name of Jesus, I loose favor, healing, restoration and answered prayers.

Daughters of Zion Prayer Series Volume 9
The Prayer Manual

I receive my spiritual, financial and material breakthrough in the mighty name of Jesus.

Pray
I thank God for the answered prayers and I soak my prayers in the blood of Jesus. I immunize my body, spirit and soul with the blood of Jesus. I come against the evil attack of the enemy concerning my prayers and this book in the name of Jesus.

By the power in the blood of Jesus, I seal every leaking hold in my spiritual armor with the blood of Jesus.

Pray in the Holy Spirit!

7

Testimonies

Revelation 12:11 (NKJV)

"And they overcame him by the blood of the Lamb and by the word of their testimony, and they did not love their lives to the death."

Plagued with high blood pressure, partially robbed of my vision, I was seriously trapped and bound to doctors' prescriptions. Satan was on his mission to destroy me from head to toe and from top to bottom. Depressed and confused, I intentionally tried to hide the real truth of my condition. Family members and friends were deceived and sometimes even outrightly fooled that I was okay and doing just fine as usual.

It was then that my sister introduced me to the Daughters of Zion Ministry. Reluctantly, I attended and defiantly I decided to sit in one corner where I could hardly be seen. When the prayer session began and Evangelist Celie,

Daughters of Zion Prayer Series Volume 9
The Prayer Manual

along with other prayer warriors, began to pray, they prayed the Word concerning healing. The anointing became evident and where there was doubt, faith took over and a transformation began in my body. I left that place feeling clean and relieved and today I am most happy to say prayer works!

My vision has returned, my blood pressure is now under control and prayer continues to work for me. Prayer is a powerful tool and an ideal weapon, particularly when uttered out of the mouths of sincere hearts. To God be the glory for all He has done for me through DZM. Thank you Lord!

— Sis Beverly

Operating in the capacity of a single parent has not been easy. My son and I have been blessed by God through the power of prayer through the Daughters of Zion Ministry. God has shown us his mighty hand of blessings and provisions. (Philippians 4:19) My son is coming into his last year of an out-of-state college and miraculously he is debt-free of any college debt, by the power of God Almighty. We now know God to a greater degree as Jehovah Jirah and as a God of true favor (Proverbs 3:1-4) because of prayer and

Daughters of Zion Prayer Series Volume 9
The Prayer Manual

keeping God's word before us. I truly know that this would not be possible without the power of touching and agreeing with others. (Matthew 18:19-20)

— Minister Wanda

DZM teaches you how to superimpose God's Kingdom over the kingdoms of this world though intercession. Evangelist Celie lays a solid foundation for overturning, overruling and overriding the satanic powers of darkness in our nation, in our families and in our churches. Like a wise prophet and a seasoned prayer warrior, she addresses the importance of thanksgiving and praise, confessions of sin, and binding strongholds. She places top priority on the atoning work of Christ on the cross by providing the biblical and commonsense tools on how to win the fight against the enemy by the authority and Lordship of Jesus Christ.

I have found the prayer points to be extremely effective in helping me prevail against the enemy's tactics and secure permanent breakthrough in my own personal life. I have seen situations concerning my son, my daughter, and my mother overturned because of the strategic prayer model found

Daughters of Zion Prayer Series Volume 9
The Prayer Manual

in her Prayer Manual. Thank you, Evangelist Celie, for sharing this book with the world. May God supply all your need according to his riches in glory by Christ Jesus. (Philippians 4:19) Amen.

— Sis BJ

Some years ago, while my daughter was away in college (in fact five hours away from home) I received a call one night that my daughter was being admitted to the hospital. I was alone at home, my husband being at work. I immediately called my elder sister and Evangelist Celie. They both prayed with me and encouraged me to stand strong in the Word.

We left home at 4:00 a.m. the next morning and at about 5:30 a.m. my phone rang and it was Evangelist Celie calling to pray with us as we journeyed. We did not knew what exactly to expect but we were sure God was with us.

On our arrival we were told she would be hospitalized for least seven to ten days. On our return home I again spoke with Evangelist Celie who promised to stand with us in agreement prayer for seven nights. She prophesied that my daughter would spend less

Daughters of Zion Prayer Series Volume 9
The Prayer Manual

than seven days in the hospital and of course that's exactly what happened. God graciously intervened and allowed my daughter to miss very little time from her classes. She has since graduated. Praise God. God answers prayers. We all need a strong prayer partner to stand with us in our hour of crisis and Evangelist Celie, along with the DZM Prayer Ministry, have a proven track record. They are reliable, dependable and faithful and will stand with you all the way. To God be the glory!
— Minister Joy

As a DZM member I've learned how to pray "strategically." Praying strategically fervently opens doors and breaks barriers. In 2015, after consistently going through so much with trying to regain a previous license, which I surrendered without success, I decided to wait on God. After almost ten years, DZM was doing an end of year prayer preparing for the New Year 2016. Evangelist Celie asked the members to declare what they wanted God to do for them and to be in expectation. Most importantly, we were given the instruction on when you pray, you must pray strategically with expectations from God. I prayed with the expectation that God would deliver the license at the beginning of January 2016. I

Daughters of Zion Prayer Series Volume 9
The Prayer Manual

started with: "Lord, I need you to move this person in this position and relocate her else where." And the Lord answered my prayers and she was moved.

The first week of January 2016, I called several times and it was just the voicemail. Afterwards, I called the Director of the Department only to be told, "She hasn't heard from her." A few days later I received a call stating that she was, "gone unexpectedly" and someone else has taken over.

In October of 2016, a license was issued to my company. God is simply amazing! Some problems or an obstacle require you to pray strategically. Today, by the grace of God, we are still licensed. I encourage you to trust God and put Him first in everything — including your business. He will not fail you.

— Nadege N. Fevry, CEO
Family Behavioral Services, LLC

Conclusion

It has been a privilege to share this DZM prayer model with you. If this book has helped you in any way, we'd loved to hear from you. Send us your testimony. I thank God for the opportunity to share with you that prayer changes everything.

If you need prayer, encouragement or just want to share with someone, please write us. We will pray for you and be in agreement with you for God's very best, or join us on our weekly prayer call.

In conclusion, when you pray, start with praise, confession of sins, binding, invite the Holy Spirit and then present your prayer request to God. He will answer you.

Daughters of Zion Prayer Series Volume 9
The Prayer Manual

Prayer of Salvation

God loves you that He gave His only begotten Son for you. The bible tells us that if you declare with your mouth that Jesus is Lord, and believe in your heart that God rose him from the dead, you will be saved, for it is with your heart that you believe and are justified and it is with your mouth that you profess your faith and are saved. (Romans 10:9-10)

If you would like to accept Jesus Christ as your Lord and Savior; first, acknowledge your sins, secondly, believe in your heart that Jesus died for you and finally, repent, confess and forsake your sins. Say the following prayer out loud and mean it from your heart.

"Heavenly Father, I come to you in the name of Jesus Christ. I believe in my heart that Jesus Christ is the son of God. I believe in my heart that he died for my sins. I believe that you raised Him from the dead for my

Daughters of Zion Prayer Series Volume 9
The Prayer Manual

justification. Lord Jesus, come into my heart right now. I receive you today as my personal Lord and Savior. I give you all the Glory."

If you have sincerely prayed this prayer, then you are now born again. Congratulations!

Daughters of Zion Prayer Series Volume 9
The Prayer Manual

About DZM

Daughters of Zion is a prophetic prayer ministry that is focused on empowering women and men who have been broken by life's challenges and then steering them to God's holy word through prayer. DZM is focused on God's holy word, the Bible, and is Holy Spirit empowered and directed. Also, DZM was founded on the Spiritual Rock, our Lord and Savior Jesus Christ, and He is also the only rock on which our ministry stands. Our charter is the Holy Bible and the Holy Spirit is our spiritual guide.

DZM coordinates a weekly conference call prayer line every Saturday from 9:00 a.m. to 10:00 a.m. United States Eastern Standard Time; a Monthly Prophetic Prayer Meeting; a Quarterly Retreat at Gilgal; and a DZM Anniversary Celebration annually in October. To participate in any of these meetings, contact us at dzmpraise@yahoo.com.

Daughters of Zion Prayer Series Volume 9
The Prayer Manual

About the Founder

Evangelist Celie is the founder of the Daughters of Zion Ministries that reaches out to men and women with their families. She is an anointed woman of God whom He has called for a time such as this. She is an inspirational speaker, life coach, an author and intercessor with a mandate to reach out to those who are hurting and broken, especially people who are simple seeking a closer relationship with God through our Lord and Savior Jesus Christ.

She is an international evangelist, a missionary and conference host. She is designed to uplift, strengthen and empower people to step into destiny and fulfill purpose. She is a wife and a mother. She traveled overseas for mission trips to: South Africa in 2011; Bahamas in 2012; Dominican Republic in 2013; Jamaica in 2014; St.Vincent in 2015; Curacao in 2016; Swaziland in 2017; St.Lucia in 2018; Jamaica 2019; and Cork Ireland for the promotion of

**Daughters of Zion Prayer Series Volume 9
The Prayer Manual**

the Healing Water Book Volume 1.

She holds a Master's Degree in Social Work (with clinical concentration and specialization in families and children) from University of Maryland, School of Social Work, in Baltimore, Maryland. She graduated from Bible School at Evangel Central Bible School in Maryland.

Her purpose and passion is to build and restore families and their relationships with God. She remains focused on her God-given, directed vision and mission. She lives her life daily as a minister of reconciliation. Her personal ministry is to intercede for families.

**Daughters of Zion Prayer Series Volume 9
The Prayer Manual**

∞∞∞∞∞∞∞∞∞∞∞♦ ♦ ♦ ♦ ♦∞∞∞∞∞∞∞∞∞∞∞

Daughters of Zion

Join the Weekly Conference Call Prayer Line

Every Saturday from 9:00 - 10:00 a.m.
(United States Eastern Standard Time)

This weekly prayer is free and we do not charge any membership fees to join DZM.

To participate in the Conference Call Prayer Line, please dial 516-597-9731.

∞∞∞∞∞∞∞∞∞∞∞♦ ♦ ♦ ♦ ♦∞∞∞∞∞∞∞∞∞∞∞